LAMINE YAMAL

THE WONDER BOY OF BARCELONA

GRETEL JONES

Disclaimer

This book contains information that is solely meant to be educational. Despite their best efforts to present accurate and current information, the author and publisher disclaim all expressed and implied representations and warranties regarding the availability, completeness, accuracy, reliability, suitability, or suitability of the content contained herein for any purpose. The publisher and the author disclaim all responsibility for any loss or harm, including without limitation, consequential or indirect loss or damage, or any loss or damage at all resulting from lost profits or data resulting from using this book.

TABLE OF CONTENT

CHAPTER 11: GLOSSARY

QUESTIONS

CHAPTER 1: MEET LAMINE: A SPECIAL BOY FROM BARCELONA

Hey there! Let's talk about a really cool kid named Lamine Yamal. Lamine is a boy who was born in Barcelona, a big and beautiful city in Spain. , he's already doing amazing things!

Lamine lives in Barcelona with his family. It's a city full of colorful buildings, yummy food, and lots of people who love soccer. In fact, Barcelona is famous for its soccer team, and Lamine is part of it!

Lamine's mom and dad noticed something special about him when he was very young. He could kick a ball better than most kids his age. He loved playing soccer in the park, at school, and even in his house.

Lamine's family comes from Morocco, a country in Africa, but Lamine was born and raised in Spain. This means he can speak different languages and enjoys foods from both places. How cool is that?

Just like you, Lamine goes to school and has homework. But he also spends a lot of time playing soccer. It's his favorite thing to do! He practices almost every day to get better and better.

What makes Lamine really special is that he started playing for one of the best soccer teams in the world when he was only 15 years old! Most players have to wait until they're much older. But Lamine worked hard and showed everyone how talented he is.

Now, people all over the world know about this boy from Barcelona. They call him a "wonder boy" because it's rare to see someone so young play so well. But remember, Lamine is just a kid like you who followed his dream and never gave up.

CHAPTER 2: LAMINE'S FIRST STEPS IN SOCCER

Let's go back in time a little bit and see how Lamine started playing soccer. It all began when he was very young, maybe even younger than you are now!

Lamine first discovered soccer when he was just a tiny kid. His dad gave him a small ball, and Lamine couldn't stop kicking it around the house. He loved the way the ball felt on his feet and how he could make it go wherever he wanted.

Soon, Lamine was playing soccer every chance he got. In the park, at school during recess, and even in the hallways at home (but shh, don't tell his parents!). His friends and family noticed that he was really good at it. He could dribble the ball better than kids much older than him!

When Lamine was about 5 years old, his parents signed him up for a local soccer team. This was super exciting for little Lamine! He got his very own uniform and learned what it was like to play on a real team.

On his first team, Lamine made new friends and learned important things about soccer. He learned how to pass the ball to his teammates, how to shoot at the goal, and how to be a good sport whether his team won or lost.

Lamine's coaches were amazed by how well he played. They would often tell his parents, "Your son has a special talent!" Lamine scored lots of goals and helped his team win many games. But the best part for Lamine was just having fun playing the game he loved.

Even back then, people could see that Lamine had something special. He wasn't just good at soccer - he seemed to understand the game in a way that most kids his age didn't. He could see where to pass the ball before anyone else, and he always seemed to be in the right place at the right time.

As Lamine got better and better, bigger soccer clubs started to notice him. They wanted him to come play for their teams. This was the beginning of an exciting journey for Lamine - one that would take him all the way to FC Barcelona, one of the best soccer teams in the world!

CHAPTER 3: LA MASIA: BARCELONA'S FAMOUS SOCCER SCHOOL

Have you ever heard of a school just for soccer? Well, that's what La Masia is! It's a special place where young players learn to become soccer stars. La Masia belongs to FC Barcelona, one of the best soccer teams in the world.

When Lamine was 7 years old, something amazing happened. FC Barcelona invited him to join La Masia! This was a big deal because not many kids get this chance. Lamine was super excited but also a little nervous.

At La Masia, Lamine's days were very different from most kids his age. He would wake up early and go to regular school classes, just like you do. But after school, instead of going home, he would train at La Masia.

Training at La Masia wasn't just about kicking a ball around. Lamine learned all sorts of things:
- How to control the ball perfectly

- The best ways to pass to teammates

- Tricks to dribble past other players

- How to shoot the ball into the goal

- Working together as a team

The coaches at La Masia were very smart. They taught Lamine not just how to play soccer, but how to think about soccer. They showed him how to see the whole field and make quick decisions.

Lamine made many friends at La Masia. All the kids there loved soccer just as much as he did. They would practice together, eat meals together, and even live together in special dorms.

But it wasn't always easy. Lamine had to work very hard. Sometimes he missed his family and his old friends. But he knew that if he wanted to become a great player, he had to keep trying his best.

As the years went by, Lamine got better and better. The coaches started to say he was one of the best players they had ever seen at La Masia. This made Lamine very proud, but it also made him want to work even harder.

La Masia wasn't just teaching Lamine how to be a good soccer player. It was teaching him how to be a good person too. He learned about teamwork, respect, and never giving up, even when things get tough.

Little did Lamine know that his time at La Masia was preparing him for something really big. Soon, he would get a chance that most kids only dream about!

CHAPTER 4: GROWING UP FAST

Lamine's soccer skills were getting better and better every day. Let's see what happened next in his amazing journey.

As Lamine got older, people started to notice something special about him. He wasn't just good at soccer - he was really, really good! Even when he played with kids who were older than him, Lamine stood out.

When Lamine was 11, he got to play in a big youth tournament. Kids from all over Spain came to play. Lamine's team did great, and guess what? Lamine scored more goals than anyone else! This made a lot of people take notice.

The coaches at Barcelona were super impressed. They decided to move Lamine up to play with older kids. This was a big challenge for Lamine. The other players were bigger and stronger than him. But Lamine didn't let that stop him!

Lamine worked extra hard to keep up with the older kids. He had to run faster, think quicker, and be braver than ever before. It wasn't always easy, but Lamine never gave up.

Soon, something amazing happened. Lamine wasn't just keeping up with the older kids - he was often better than them! He could dribble past them, make clever passes, and score amazing goals.

The big bosses at Barcelona couldn't believe what they were seeing. They started to wonder if Lamine might be ready for something even bigger. Could this young boy be good enough to play with the grown-ups?

Lamine kept working hard and improving. He watched videos of great players to learn new tricks. He practiced his shooting and passing every chance he got. He even worked on getting stronger so he could keep up with bigger players.

All of Lamine's hard work was about to pay off in a big way. The coaches of Barcelona's first team - the one with all the famous adult players - started to pay attention to this young wonder boy.

Lamine was growing up fast, not just in how tall he was getting, but in how good he was at soccer. He was on his way to making history, and he was still just a kid!

Little did Lamine know that very soon, he would get a chance that most soccer players can only dream about.

CHAPTER 5: MAKING HISTORY: LAMINE'S BIG MOMENTS

Lamine was about to do something amazing! At just 15 years old, he got a chance that most soccer players only dream about.

First, Lamine played for Barcelona B. This is like the junior team for the big Barcelona club. He was the youngest player ever to do this! Everyone was surprised to see such a young boy playing so well against grown-ups.

But that was just the start. A few months later, something even more incredible happened. The coach of the main Barcelona team asked Lamine to play with them. Can you believe it? At 15, Lamine was going to play with some of the best soccer players in the world!

On April 29, 2023, Lamine stepped onto the field wearing the famous Barcelona shirt. The crowd cheered as he became the youngest player ever to play for

Barcelona in a league game. Lamine wasn't nervous - he was excited!

Lamine didn't just play; he played really well. He helped his team and almost scored a goal. Everyone watching was amazed. They knew they were seeing something special.

After the game, people all over the world were talking about Lamine. Newspapers, TV shows, and websites all wanted to tell his story. Lamine had made history, and he was still just a kid like you!

This was just the beginning of Lamine's big adventure in professional soccer. He showed everyone that with hard work and talent, even young people can do amazing things.

CHAPTER 6: LAMINE'S PLAYING STYLE: WHAT MAKES HIM SPECIAL?

Let's talk about what makes Lamine such a great soccer player. He has some really cool skills that make him stand out on the field.

First, Lamine is super fast! He can run past other players like they're standing still. This helps him get away from defenders and find space to play.

Lamine is also really good at dribbling. That means he can control the ball while running. He uses quick little touches to keep the ball close to his feet. It's like the ball is stuck to his shoes!

One of Lamine's favorite tricks is called "La Croqueta." It's a movie where he quickly moves the ball from one foot to the other to get past defenders. It's tricky and fun to watch!

Lamine is left-footed, which means he's best at kicking with his left foot. But he's been practicing with his right foot too, so he can shoot and pass with both feet.

On the field, Lamine usually plays on the right side of the attack. From there, he can cut inside and shoot with his strong left foot. He's also great at passing to his teammates when they're in a good position to score.

What makes Lamine really special is how he thinks about the game. He seems to know what's going to happen before it does. This helps him make smart decisions really quickly.

Lamine isn't very big, but he uses his size to his advantage. He can turn quickly and squeeze through small spaces between defenders.

All these skills together make Lamine a really exciting player to watch. He's always trying new things and surprising everyone with what he can do!

CHAPTER 7: LIFE AS A YOUNG PRO

Being a young soccer star is cool, but it's not always easy. Let's see what Lamine's life is like now.

Lamine still goes to school, just like you do. But he has to work extra hard to keep up with his classes because he spends so much time playing soccer. He often does homework on the bus or in between training sessions.

Training with the Barcelona team is tough. Lamine practices almost every day. He has to eat healthy foods and go to bed early to stay strong and fit. Sometimes, this means he can't hang out with friends as much as he'd like to.

Lamine now has some new grown-up things to think about. He has to be careful about what he says in interviews and how he acts in public. Lots of kids look up to him now, so he tries to set a good example.

Fame can be tricky. Lamine is recognized on the street sometimes, and people ask for his autograph or selfies. This is fun, but it can also be a bit overwhelming for a young person.

Lamine also has to deal with pressure. When he plays in big games, thousands of people are watching. He has to stay calm and do his best, even when he's nervous.

Despite all these challenges, Lamine still loves playing soccer more than anything. He knows he's lucky to be living his dream at such a young age.

Lamine has a lot of support from his family, teammates, and coaches. They help him balance his soccer life with being a regular kid. This support is really important for Lamine.

Even though his life is different from most kids his age, Lamine still finds time to have fun, play video games, and hang out with friends when he can. He's learning that being a soccer star is about finding the right balance in life.

CHAPTER 8: DREAMS AND GOALS

Lamine has already done some amazing things, but he's got big dreams for the future!

One of Lamine's biggest dreams is to become a regular starter for FC Barcelona. He wants to play in every game and help his team win lots of trophies. Lamine dreams of scoring goals in important matches and hearing the crowd cheer his name.

Another big goal for Lamine is to play for Spain's national team. This is the team that represents the whole country in big tournaments like the World Cup. Lamine hopes to wear the red shirt of Spain one day and make his country proud.

Lamine looks up to other soccer stars for inspiration. He watches videos of players like Lionel Messi and Ronaldinho, trying to learn from their amazing skills. Lamine hopes that one day, kids will look up to him the same way.

Off the field, Lamine has dreams too. He wants to finish his education and maybe even go to college someday. He knows that being smart is just as important as being good at soccer.

Lamine also wants to use his fame to help others. He dreams of starting a charity to help kids who don't have the same opportunities he had. He wants to build soccer fields in poor neighborhoods and give out free soccer equipment.

But Lamine knows that dreams don't come true by themselves. He works hard every day to get better and better. He practices extra, listens to his coaches, and never gives up, even when things get tough.

Lamine's biggest dream is to be remembered as one of the best soccer players ever. But he also wants to be known as a good person who inspires others to follow their dreams.

CHAPTER 9: OFF THE FIELD: LAMINE'S EVERYDAY LIFE

Even though Lamine is a soccer star, he's still a kid like you in many ways. Let's peek into what he does when he's not playing soccer!

Lamine loves video games, just like many of you do. His favorite game is FIFA, where he can play with soccer teams from around the world. Sometimes, he even plays as himself in the game, which he thinks is pretty cool!

Music is another big part of Lamine's life. He likes listening to different types of music, especially when he's getting ready for a big game. It helps him relax and feel pumped up at the same time.

Lamine spends a lot of time with his family. They're his biggest supporters and help keep him grounded. He enjoys having dinner with them and telling them about his day. His mom still makes his favorite Moroccan dishes, which reminds him of his roots.

Friends are important to Lamine too. He has buddies from school and from the soccer academy. When he has free time, he likes to hang out with them, watch movies, or just chat and laugh together.

Lamine is interested in fashion and likes to dress well. He enjoys picking out cool outfits, especially sneakers. Sometimes, he even gets to wear clothes from famous brands because he's becoming well-known.

To relax, Lamine likes to read books about other athletes and their journeys.

He finds their stories inspiring and learns from their experiences.

Lamine also tries to give back to his community. He visits children's hospitals and soccer schools for kids who don't have many opportunities. He remembers when he was a young kid dreaming of playing soccer and wants to inspire others.

Even with all the excitement in his life, Lamine still has to do regular kid stuff like chores at home and homework. His parents make sure he stays humble and doesn't forget the importance of education.

Despite being famous, Lamine tries to live a normal life as much as possible. He knows that being a good person is just as important as being a good soccer player.

CHAPTER 10: FUN FACTS ABOUT LAMINE'S

1. Favorite Food: Lamine loves his mom's homemade couscous. It's a tasty dish from Morocco that makes him feel at home.

2. Lucky Number: Lamine's favorite number is 27. That's the number on his jersey when he plays for Barcelona!

3. Languages: Lamine can speak three languages - Spanish, Catalan, and Arabic. How cool is that?

4. Nickname: His teammates sometimes call him "El Pequeño" which means "The Little One" in Spanish, because he's younger than most of them.

5. Video Game Champion: Lamine is really good at FIFA video games. He often wins when he plays against his friends!

6. First Soccer Ball: Lamine still has the first soccer ball his dad gave him when he

was little. He keeps it as a special memory.

7. Funny Moment: Once during practice, Lamine accidentally kicked the ball into a bucket of water. Everyone laughed, including Lamine!

8. Favorite Subject: In school, Lamine really enjoys math. He says it helps him think quickly on the soccer field too.

9. Soccer Hero: Lamine looks up to Lionel Messi. He even got to meet Messi once and was super excited!

10. Pre-game Ritual: Before every game, Lamine ties his left shoe first. He thinks it brings him good luck.

11. Dream Vacation: Lamine would love to visit Japan someday. He thinks their soccer stadiums look amazing!

12. Favorite Celebration: When Lamine scores a goal, he likes to do a little dance. His teammates think it's really funny.

CHAPTER 11: GLOSSARY

1. Assist: When a player passes the ball to a teammate who then scores a goal.

2. Corner Kick: A kick taken from the corner of the field when the ball goes out of bounds off the defending team.

3. Dribble: Moving the ball along the ground with your feet while running.

4. Free Kick: A kick awarded to a team when the other team breaks a rule.

5. Goal: When the ball goes into the net. It's how teams score points!

6. Header: When a player hits the ball with their head, usually to pass or shoot.

7. Offside: A tricky rule that means an attacking player can't be closer to the goal than the defenders when the ball is passed to them.

8. Penalty Kick: A free shot at the goal given when a serious foul happens in the penalty area.

9. Red Card: A card the referee shows to send a player out of the game for a very bad foul.

10. Save: When the goalkeeper stops the ball from going into the goal.

11. Striker: A player whose main job is to score goals.

12. Tackle: When a player tries to take the ball away from an opponent.

13. Yellow Card: A warning card the referee shows for a less serious foul.

14. Pitch: Another word for the soccer field.

15. La Masia: The special soccer school where Lamine learned to play for Barcelona.

16. Nutmeg: When a player kicks the ball between an opponent's legs.

17. Hat-trick: When a player scores three goals in one game.

18. Referee: The person in charge of making sure players follow the rules during a game.

19. Midfielder: A player who plays in the middle of the field, helping both attack and defense.

20. Defender: A player whose main job is to stop the other team from scoring.

21. Stoppage Time: Extra minutes added at the end of each half to make up for pauses in play.

22. Bicycle Kick: A fancy move where a player kicks the ball while doing a backflip.

23. Clean Sheet: When a team doesn't let the other team score any goals in a game.

24. Throw-in: How players restart the game when the ball goes out of bounds on the sidelines.

25. Captain: The player chosen to be the team leader on the field.

26. Offside Trap: When defenders move up the field together to make attacking players offside.

27. Wall: A line of defending players standing together to block a free kick.

28. Chip Shot: When a player softly kicks the ball in a high arc over the goalkeeper.

29. Derby: A match between two teams from the same city or area.

30. Volley: Kicking the ball while it's still in the air and hasn't touched the ground.

QUESTIONS

1. How old was Lamine when he first played for Barcelona's main team?

2. What is the name of Barcelona's famous soccer school where Lamine trained?

3. Can you name two languages that Lamine speaks?

4. What is Lamine's favorite video game?

5. What number does Lamine wear on his jersey?

6. What position does Lamine usually play on the field?

7. Can you remember one of Lamine's tips for young players?

8. What is Lamine's favorite food?

9. Name one challenge Lamine faces as a young professional player.

10. What does Lamine do to relax when he's not playing soccer?

11. Who is one soccer player that Lamine looks up to?

12. What is "La Croqueta" and why is it special to Lamine?

13. Can you explain what an "assist" is in soccer?

14. What does Lamine dream of doing in the future besides playing for Barcelona?

15. How does Lamine try to give back to his community?

Made in the USA
Las Vegas, NV
14 October 2024

96823502R00036